STRAIGHT FROM THE HEART

STRAIGHT FROM THE HEART

MARY K. JOHNSON

SPEAKING VOLUMES, LLC

NAPLES, FLORIDA

2011

STRAIGHT FROM THE HEART

ISBN 978-1-61232-038-0

Table of Contents

Happy Endings

While I was blind,
then came to see
it was my second chance
I was not mocked
by the Lord,
nor was I judged,
or blamed.
He understood
when I did err,
and so he pardoned me.

No Time to Waste

With no desire
for worldly goods,
which only blocks the way,
instead my focus
was on the Lord,
he who would care for me.

All in Advance

It is a scene
of scattered pieces
a mere vision
of my life
taking its refuge
at the back
of my mind
a constant reminder
of the choices
I must make
from a mass
of many
twists and turns,
I will choose
only one route,
that is to be the one I take.

At Ease

And when my burdens
were taken from me,
leaving my heart content,
I dropped to my knees
just as always,
for I had to thank the Lord.

Beware

Some may often wonder,
which road would be the best.
We shall know soon enough,
once we're put to the test.

Be not quick at doing wrong,
we have choices we can make.
Take time and think it through,
and think right for goodness sake.

Your road is rough as you make it,
or as easy as can be.
Good or bad, you choose it.
Do right and be set free.

Evils lurks in dark places,
where the righteous dare to go.
The righteous must know something,
a sinner does not know.

Let's all get it together.
Let's all try and meet there.
Let's meet at the straight and narrow,
not that road which is labeled **BEWARE**!

Day Dreaming

I'd like to be alone to dream,
then things would go my way.
I'd set things the way I want,
and that's how they would stay.

I'm happier when I dream,
because here there is no pain,
as long as things go my way,
Here's where I'll remain.

In my dreams you may be there,
that's something I must decide.
In this place I am boss.
Here only I abide.

There's no pressure here,
my mind is free to roam,
if I didn't have to wake,
this place would be my home.

Here I can't be rejected,
no one here to break my heart.
Here is the best place for me.
Here I can make a fresh start.

Elevation

Who we are
and strive to be
is shown
in all we do
year after year,
step after step,
continue being persistent
with feet on solid ground,
making this
your stepping stone
while reaching
greater lengths.

Love at First Sight

It was through you,
that I first learned
what love truly is,
and when I did,
it was you, mom,
that I first loved,
because you were always
there for me.

Serenity

A peaceful place, oh land of God,
a place to feel that I belong.

Nothing else can compare,
to a place that feels like home.

Now I See

We think
we know
all that we should,
until the day is done,
and with each day
a lesson's learned,
of what
we did not know.

On Your Feet

And I shall say,
when I am seen
with a smile upon my face,
it was the Lord,
when I was down,
who raised me to my feet,
and I am glad even more,
that with loving hands,
he supports me still.

Pain, Pain, Go Away

Pain has no feelings
no conscious, no concern,
and cares not of the consequences,
of how its sting does burn.

Pain hears no pleads,
no words to block its' way,
and will not give answers
to anything you say.

Pain has no sympathy
to soothe the aching heart.
It's gone before you know it
and leaves us torn apart.

Pain knows not the depth
of the trouble it relays,
and cares not the length
of how long it stays.

Pain has no direction,
has no eyes to see.
Asks not what our names are,
before it makes its flee.

Pain you are not welcome here
I say to you once more.
I need more time for mending,
you've been here once before.

Phase Two

There are things
life offers us
like fun and games
and such,
then comes the time
when that all ends,
and nothing else matters
except romance.

Precious Love

While you held me,
and rocked me,
and sang me lullabies,
I knew not who you were,
but now I know,
you are my mom,
and I love you
even more.

Tender Hearts

The heart is like a child,
it must receive great care.
It must not be ignored,
as if it isn't there.

The heart should be protected,
guarded against misdeeds.
It should be treated special,
and given what it needs.

No heart should be broken,
it should receive no pain.
It should not be subjected,
to any kind of strain.

If intentions are misguided,
the heart would surely know.
It, too, becomes a victim,
it, too, receives a blow.

So, avoid taking risks,
for which the heart will pay.
Keep watch over your hearts,
send trouble on its' way.

A Love So Great

Just as light
about my life,
that which helps me see,
the air, also,
I need to breathe,
my warmth
when I am cold,
you have been
my everything, mom,
and I have loved you so.

Ready, Set, Go

Though I may feel
I am prepared
to go take on
the world,
I can be sure
that I will know,
in just a matter
of time.

Destiny

There's no planning, no plotting,
it's as natural as can be.
There are no warning signs,
and no way to foresee.

There's no particular time,
no particular date.
No particular reason
to sit around and wait.

There's no speaking with the God's,
to learn of what's to come.
Look only for the best there is,
care less of where it's from.

There are no choices to be made,
this is no lottery,
this is no game at all,
this is your destiny.

Good fortune we except,
with bad we can't relate.
We must all acknowledge,
that it's all a part of fate.

For the Love of Kin

Who else
is there,
in this world
whom I could
love more
than my dad.
There is no one
at all,
other than him
of course.

Love Connection

Not only
by genetics
are we linked
together, dad,
but most importantly,
we are bonded together
by love.

A Family Affair

Like grains of sand, we are alike,
connected from where it began.
My mother and father came together,
and gave much life to their land.

We are family, joined by our blood,
which extended from the love of two.
Mother and father, and a plan they made,
was well played out, and it grew.

Who we are now, is part of a dream,
a vision that had come to be.
Yes, Mom and Dad, like a storybook tale,
made us what they wanted to see.

We are still here to carry on,
like a role in a part to play.
We are the dream which came,
from my mother and father one day.

So never forget where you come from,
never forget family and friends.
Don't forget me, "the poet".
Never forget your kin.

It's Love Either Way

If I could somehow
be the father,
and you, dad,
could be me,
you'd see firsthand
the great job
you've done,
at making me to be
who I am,
and for that particular reason,
I would not change a thing,
and that,
is because you are the best.

Loved in Return

My thanks to you, dad,
for the many years
that you have been
such a loving father,
and thanks, also, for being,
my closest and dearest friend.

Laying it on the Line

There's no doubt about it,
while I'm in this world,
my standards will not drop,
I'm not that sort of girl.

I'm not some easy prey,
I know what I should know,
I also have a limit,
to how far this girl will go.

I have guidelines to follow,
each and every day,
without them I am lost,
I'm the one who'll pay.

I've done quite well so far,
because I stand my ground,
I'll except no disrespect,
I'll not be pushed around.

Do not get me wrong,
it's not that I'm unfair,
I simply must be careful,
it's a cold, cold world out there.

Smooth Sailing

Impressively
you went about
on your own
from day to day
being not swayed
by anyone,
in need of no demands.
How proud I am
that you've come out on top,
regardless of blocks in your paths.

Taking Control

Whatsoever my destiny,
that which is unknown,
nothing of this world
can take it away from me.

What Happiness Is

Who's to say what happiness is,
who really knows for sure?
Is it a day at the races,
or something much more pure?

Does happiness touch the heart,
much like a newborn child,
or is it something else,
like weeds growing wild?

Does it keep you with a smile,
constantly, day to day,
or is it another ball game,
once the rain has gone away?

Is happiness some state of mind,
or something that we feel,
or is it some fantasy,
or something much more real?

Is happiness kin to love,
does it make us apt to give?
Does it have any affect,
on the way we live?

Happiness is that and more,
and I am glad to say,
that as long as I am happy,
happy is how I'll stay!

Agape

For many years
your love has been
as my direction,
of which I appreciate,
it, too, has been
as a lesson well learned,
my guide,
and my support.
So as I follow
in your footsteps,
so I shall surely
pass it on.

A Job Well Done

However one manages
to accomplish a goal
just as you have done,
a show is made
of who you are
in your efforts to succeed,
and for that very reason
you are one
who has become
worthy of much praise.

Aglow

Brightly it shone,
and far away,
it changed the earth,
from night to day.

It was no star, no UFO,
most unusual it seemed.
"Is this some message to me,"
I wondered as it beamed.

My heart missing beats,
I was surrounded by light,
frightened beyond belief,
not a rescuer in sight.

"Has time come to an end,
have they come for me?"
Please dim your lights,
then I can see.

Then I thought leaving the yard,
frightened by lights on a chopper,
"should I tell anyone I was spooked,
by lights on a police helicopter."

Days Gone By

It's no longer like it was,
those days gone by.
Time will not rewind itself,
there'll be no need to try.

So much time has taken,
gone without a trace.
Only memories of our past,
keeps those days in place.

The love, the happiness,
the pain and the tears,
that was also a part,
of those long ago years.

Tomorrow will leave memories,
today will leave them also.
Regardless of what day it is,
they'll simply come and go.

Time takes so much from us,
yet leaves as much behind.
Deep inside our yesterdays,
amidst our hearts and minds.

Going Up

Each beginning has an end,
but first where does it start.
Focus wisely on the role,
of which you'll play the part.

Let no obstacles block you,
fight hard to succeed.
Failure can come easily,
that you do not need.

It may at times seem scary,
but who am I to say.
A coward has no backbone,
they'll run the other way.

Who and what we are,
and that which we'll achieve,
is who we will become,
if only we believe.

Focus straight ahead,
by now it should be clear,
success is our dream,
of what we hold most dear.

Easy Street

Got to go to easy street,
that's the place to be.
The vibes are positive there,
no signs of misery.

Got to go to easy street,
the place with class and style.
A friendly, peaceful atmosphere,
the trip will be worthwhile.

Got to go to easy street
it's no confusion there.
It'll be no crooked deals,
all is treated fair.

Got to go to easy street,
It is no evil there,
no swindling, no jealously,
It'll be no burdens to bare.

Got to go to easy street,
where big bucks do not rule.
If I did not go there,
then that would not be cool!

A Second Chance

Dear father am I worthy,
may I have a second chance?
From trouble I'll break away,
I'll not give it another glance.

It's not whether to win or lose,
but the means to a positive end,
which can only be accomplished,
by steering clear of sin.

Just ask of whomever's been there,
and of those who understand,
if life should not be valued,
by all who dwells in this land.

There's just enough time to prepare
and just enough time to change.
Don't wait until the last minute,
don't get to far out of range.

Be sure not to have regrets,
be sure to stay in control.
Don't have to suffer the consequences,
and don't say that you haven't been told.

Turn Around

There is no more wondering,
I see it clearly now,
What I thought was gone,
has returned again somehow.

A journey it was, a very long trip,
no returning there anymore.
I'd become some other person,
whom I'd never known before.

If I'd known from the start,
that it all was a waste for me,
I'd ventured too far away,
and could no longer see.

Welcome back, I tell myself,
I'm back where I belong.
I searched for something of meaning,
while it was part of me all along.

"Are you blind, do you not see?"
You're going the wrong way.
If you cannot see it now,
I hope that you will, someday!

Black History

Please don't take away
my freedom mastuh suh
the one need I have
to roam about,
nor sell my young ones
to the rich folks
of this world,
for a handsome fee,
such as which mine eyes
have never been so
blessed enough to
set sight upon,
and might never will,
cause this is my way of life,
no better, no worse.

The Birthday Girl

You've set your goal
and let me say,
"you have done quite well,
in every way."

You're more than a sister,
you're a great friend, too.
There is so much,
that I learned from you.

You taught me how
to get all I can,
to rely on the Lord,
the aide of his hands.

You deserve to celebrate,
enjoy and have fun.
It's your due reward,
for all that you've done.

So be your pretty lil' self,
smile your pretty lil' smile,
and I hope your happiness
will last for awhile!

Role Model

I've made up my mind,
I know what I'll do.
When I'm grown up,
I'll be just like you.
You've always been kind,
considerate, too.
When I'm grown up,
I'll be just like you.
A picture of perfection,
do believe me, it's true.
When I'm grown up,
I'll be just like you.

Such grace, and such style,
you've never seemed blue.
When I'm grown up,
I'll be just like you.

I'm hung up on you,
I'm stuck just like glue.
When I'm grown up,
I'll be just like you.
Your saintly qualities.
I watched as we grew.
And when I'm grown up,
I'll be just like you.
I know you're my sisters,
still this is your due.
When I grow up,
I'll be just like you.

Tranquility

Thinking of a far away place,
unlike any ever seen.
A place where all is perfect,
fit for kings and queens.

Someplace to drift about,
like a ship lost at sea.
And all things are possible,
so how could this not be.

This longing will not go away,
it has only just begun,
there has to be someplace,
though seemingly there's none.

The quiet deserts of sand,
a farm amongst the hills.
Whatever it may take,
this hunt will be fulfilled.

Wherever it might be,
it could be on the moon.
The plan is to get there,
preferably real soon.

The Beholder

Beauty comes in many forms,
depending on what you see.
I see things for what they are,
whatever I want it to be.

There are two sides to everything,
just as day from night.
But what I cannot see in darkness,
" I see better in the light. "

VISIT

SPEAKING VOLUMES ON-LINE

National Best-Selling

&

Award Winning Authors

www.speakingvolumes.us